D0646494

MARINES

SPECIAL FORCES: PROTECTING, BUILDING, TEACHING, AND FIGHTING

AIR FORCE

ARMY RANGERS

ELITE FORCES SELECTION

ESCAPE AND EVASION

GREEN BERETS

MARINES

NAVY SEALS

URBAN WARFARE

PARACHUTE REGIMENT

WORLD'S BEST SOLDIERS

MARINES

by Jack Montana

Mason Crest Publishers

MASON CREST PUBLISHERS INC.
370 Reed Road
Broomall, Pennsylvania 19008
(866)MCP-BOOK (toll free)
www.masoncrest.com

First Printing
9 8 7 6 5 4 3 2 1

Library of Congress Cataloging-in-Publication Data

Montana, Jack.
  Marines / by Jack Montana.
    p. cm. — (Special forces : protecting, building, teaching and fighting)
  Includes bibliographical references and index.
  ISBN 978-1-4222-1842-6   ISBN (series) 978-1-4222-1836-5
  1. United States. Marine Corps—Juvenile literature. I. Title.
  VE23.M58 2011
  359.9'60973—dc22
                                    2010020681

Produced by Harding House Publishing Service, Inc.
www.hardinghousepages.com
Interior design by MK Bassett-Harvey.
Cover design by Torque Advertising + Design.
Printed in USA by Bang Printing.

With thanks and appreciation to the U.S. Military for the use of information, text, and images.

Contents

Introduction

Elite forces are the tip of Freedom's spear. These small, special units are universally the first to engage, whether on reconnaissance missions into denied territory for larger conventional forces or in direct action, surgical operations, preemptive strikes, retaliatory action, and hostage rescues. They lead the way in today's war on terrorism, the war on drugs, the war on transnational unrest, and in humanitarian operations as well as nation building. When large-scale warfare erupts, they offer theater commanders a wide variety of unique, unconventional options.

Most such units are regionally oriented, acclimated to the culture and conversant in the languages of the areas where they operate. Since they deploy to those areas regularly, often for combined training exercises with indigenous forces, these elite units also serve as peacetime "global scouts," and "diplomacy multipliers," beacons of hope for the democratic aspirations of oppressed peoples all over the globe.

Elite forces are truly "quiet professionals": their actions speak louder than words. They are self-motivated, self-confidant, versatile, seasoned, mature individuals who rely on teamwork more than daring-do. Unfortunately, theirs is dangerous work. Since the 1980 attempt to rescue hostages from the U.S. embassy in Tehran, American special operations forces have suffered casualties in real-world operations at close to fifteen times the rate of U.S. conventional forces. By the very nature of the challenges that face special operations forces, training for these elite units has proven even more hazardous.

Thus it's with special pride that I join you in saluting the brave men who volunteer to serve in and support these magnificent units and who face such difficult challenges ahead.

—Colonel John T. Carney, Jr., USAF–Ret.
President, Special Operations Warrior Foundation

CHAPTER 1
History of the Marine Corps

"For over 221 years our Corps has done two things for this great nation," stated General Charles C. Krulak. "We make Marines, and we win battles."

In the nineteenth century, the United States Marine Corps adopted the famous motto, *Semper Fidelis*, which is Latin for "always faithful." During their history, the Marines have always stayed tough-as-nails, seeing some of the harshest military conflict in American history. There were dark times but they have remained "always faithful." The Marines fought next to other military branches from the beginning.

Currently, the Marines are the largest elite unit in the world. In relation to other countries in the west, the Marines

HEROES: JOHN MACKIE

During the Civil War, Corporal John Mackie was the first Marine to be awarded the highest military award, the Medal of Honor. On the USS *Galena* at the battle of Drewry's Bluff, while heavy fire from Confederate forces killed or wounded much of the crew, Mackie risked his life leading the gun operation for the remainder of the battle.

dwarf any other special military force. In fact, the Marines are currently larger than the entire British army.

The Marine Corps formed in 1775. From the beginning of America's independence, the Marines acted as a defensive combat force that defended a ship's officers from **mutiny** and protected the crew. They were also established to perform **amphibious** raids. The first amphibious attack occurred early in the Revolutionary War when the Marines took over a British ammunition depot and naval port in New Providence, Bahamas. The Marines were active in defending the United States against Barbary pirates in the nineteenth century. They also performed admirably in the War of 1812 and played a role in the Civil War.

During World War I, over 13,000 Marines were killed or wounded in the trenches. Between the world wars, Marines

UNDERSTAND THE FULL MEANING

mutiny: An action against authority in which the orders of a superior are disobeyed.

amphibious: Operating in land or in water

were sent to defend the Pacific Islands. Small units were on these islands when Japanese bombers attacked the U.S. Pacific Fleet at Pearl Harbor on December 7, 1941. The subsequent Japanese offensive in the southwest Pacific captured most of New Guinea and part of the Solomon Islands. America had been taken by surprise. They began a huge fight to push the Japanese back to their homeland. The Marines were asked to help capture the Pacific Islands from the Japanese, and in doing so, they fought in some of the bloodiest battles of World War II. Iwo Jima (February to May 1945), for example, was bought with the lives of 6,800 Marines and 900 sailors, and another 20,000 were wounded.

In 1947, the National Security Act defined the three primary areas of responsibility for the Marines: "The seizure of defense of advanced naval bases and other land operations to support naval campaigns; the development of tactics, technique, and equipment used by amphibious landing forces; and such other duties as the President may direct." The Security Act defined the Marines' mission as we know it now. The Marines have used the potential of the Navy to transport forces quickly in foreign wars. The Marines may be trained for aquatic combat, but the majority of operations they have done in major wars have been on land.

HEROES: OPHA MAE JOHNSON

Although women weren't allowed in war zones during World War I, Opha Mae Johnson and 300 others proudly served, helping the Marines win in France. Today, women continue to serve in the Marines.

HEROES: LEWIS B. "CHESTY" PULLER

Lieutenant Puller earned more military decorations than any Marine in history. He guided the Marines in the battle of Inchon and the Battle of Chosin Reservoir. Lt. Puller went on nineteen campaigns. He was known to give witty quotes during battle, once stating, "They are in front of us, behind us, and we are flanked on both sides by an enemy that outnumbers us 29:1. They can't get away from us now!"

Even when World War II was over, the Marines did not rest for long. By 1950, they were back in action in the Korean War, helping to stop South Korea from being overrun by a **communist** invasion from North Korea. By now, the Marines' toughness was becoming legendary. In one particular incident, on September 26, 1950, a large force of North Korean tanks and self-propelled guns attacked the positions of the First Marine Regiment. Despite a ferocious enemy onslaught, the Marines halted the attack, in the process destroying seven tanks and killing over 500 enemy soldiers.

Some twelve years later, the Marines were again involved in a war in the Far East: Vietnam. Here again, the Marines

UNDERSTAND THE FULL MEANING

communist: A government that closely controls the economic freedom, and often other rights, of its citizens.

deployed: Military forces moved into an area of conflict.

were used to try to stop communists from North Vietnam taking over South Vietnam. The Marines fought some of the biggest battles of the entire war, as well as participating in special missions. Vietnam was the longest war in which the Marines were engaged. The Marines **deployed** more troops in Vietnam than in World War II, making Vietnam was one of the most important conflicts for the Marines. One characteristic about the Marines was evident here as

During Operation Georgia, Marines destroyed the bunkers and tunnels used by the Viet Cong to strike against U.S. forces.

HEROES: DAN DALY

Few Marines earn the Medal of Honor; even fewer could say they received two. Sergeant Major Dan Daly defended his Marines' position against Chinese snipers while they waited for reinforcements. He later earned the Medal of Honor.

Fifteen years later, in 1915, he earned the medal a second time. During the Haitian Occupation he fended off bandits during nighttime combat and defeated them by the morning. Major Smedley Butler—the only other Marine to be awarded two Medals of Honor—called him "the fightingest Marine I ever knew."

much as it had ever been: they would never surrender. In fact, most Marines would be prepared to die rather than lose a fight.

The Vietnam War ended in 1975, but the Marines did not have to wait long before they were back in action. They returned to their **expeditionary** role in the military, performing military operations abroad, often missions that were not tied to a formal war. The Marines participated in the attempted rescue of American hostages in Iran during 1980. In October 1983, they were part of a force that went in to rescue over 1,000 U.S. citizens from the small Caribbean island of Grenada. October 1983 saw the largest loss of Marines in history with the bombing of Beirut, Lebanon.

UNDERSTAND THE FULL MEANING

expeditionary: Military forces deployed in a foreign country.

In 1990, the U.S. Marines were part of the Allied forces that liberated the country of Kuwait in the Middle East from the occupation of invading soldiers from Iraq.

In September 2001, in response to terrorist attacks on New York and Washington, D.C., the Marines were put on the highest level of military alert since the Cuban Missile Crisis of 1962. After the events of 9/11, President Bush set forth the military's mission on the War on Terror: "the defeat

Lance Corporal Naoto Nakamura, a scout team leader with Charlie Company, First Light Armored Reconnaissance Battalion scans a village on the other side of a canal. C Company Marines patrolled the villages and open terrain near Parghee Bagat to identify trends in the day-to-day lives of local Afghans.

of Al-Qaeda, other terrorist groups and any nation that supports or harbors terrorists".

The war in Afghanistan was the first major operation after the 9/11 attacks. As with many other important events in American history, the Marines played an important role. During Operation Enduring Freedom, the Marines were the first **conventional** military unit used. The Marines helped other branches of the military uproot the Taliban. And they were used in various missions during the conflict.

President George W. Bush stated that, "Our war on terror begins with al Qaeda, but it does not end there." From the beginning, he thought of the War on Terror as a global operation fighting **extremism** wherever it was. In the 2003 Operation Iraqi Freedom, the Marines took part in the invasion of Iraq. They left the country in the summer of 2003 and then returned to do various missions in 2004. In 2007 President Bush sent a **surge** of troops into Iraq, which secured the country and reduced the violence there. In January 2010, the Marines officially ended participation in the Iraq war, a part of President Obama's plan to rapidly reduce the number of active troops in Iraq.

UNDERSTAND THE FULL MEANING

conventional: A regular, rather than a Special Forces, branch of the military.

extremism: A form of radical politics or religion that engages in acts of terrorism and violence.

surge: An increase in troop numbers, strength, and activity.

humanitarian: Those actions with the goal of bringing aid and assistance to a civilian population.

HEROES: JASON DUNHAM

The United States awarded Corporal Jason Dunham with the first Medal of Honor given to a Marine since the Vietnam War. During a reconnaissance mission in Karaballah, Iraq, Corporal Dunham heard gunfire nearby. He ordered his squad toward the fighting, where they discovered seven vehicles scrambling to depart. An insurgent leapt out and released a grenade. Cpl. Jason tore his helmet off and used it to cover the grenade. He died in the explosion, saving at least two other lives.

The Marines have been used in every armed conflict in which America has participated. Today, the Marine Corps is used all over the world to protect or keep the peace in many countries that are blighted by violence or war. Not only do the Marines still train to fight hard, they also perform **humanitarian** operations: distributing food to the starving and protecting people who are afraid of violence. Marines are truly special people. This is why it is so tough to get into the U.S. Marine Corps. One minute they might be in a heavy firefight with the enemy, blazing away with rifles and machine guns. The next minute they might be giving first aid to wounded civilians or taking care of children lost in a war zone.

Clearly, Marines must be as tough mentally as they are physically. In this book, you will find out just what sort of mind the U.S. Marine must have if he or she is to maintain over 100 years of proud tradition.

CHAPTER 2

Preparing to Be a Marine

**N**ot everyone is allowed to be a Marine. To join this **elite** unit, you have to show that you have the right character and intelligence to fight for the reputation of the Marine Corps. The U.S. Marine is one of the most highly trained soldiers in the world. An average Marine must be courageous, intelligent, able to make decisions quickly, capable of leading men or women into action, good at communicating, writing, and mathematics, and also be able to handle all the weapons at his or her disposal. Because so much is required, trying to get into the Marines is incredibly difficult. We will look at the recruitment process in the next chapter. Here we will see what mental qualities you need to belong to one of the world's best units.

UNDERSTAND THE FULL MEANING

elite: The best and most selective.

INTELLIGENCE

All soldiers must display intelligence, but those in elite units must have a higher than average intelligence. This makes the members of the Marine Corps excellent at working out problems and making decisions on the battlefield. Also, military psychologists have studied how intelligence affects the way people fight. They discovered that people who really threw themselves into battle were generally more intelligent than those who did not. They were also better at working out **tactics** that could win battles. In the elite units like the Marine Corps, an intelligent mind is a must.

SELF-CONTROL

To be a Marine, you have to be able to discipline yourself. This means doing dangerous, long, boring, or difficult jobs without complaining, and also doing them to the best of your ability. Elite units tend to work in small squads or even as individuals. This means that all soldiers must be able to do their jobs because other people's lives depend on them. A soldier's own self-control could be the only thing that makes a mission a success. Elite forces also spend more time watching and waiting than fighting. They must also be able to deal with the crushing boredom of long, solitary watches while staying alert.

UNDERSTAND THE FULL MEANING

tactics: Methods used in achieving a successful outcome.

Staff Sgt. Jeff Foret, a reconnaissance team leader with 1st Reconnaissance Battalion, 1st Marine Division, I Marine Expeditionary Force, lands safely after jumping from a CH-53E "Super Stallion" during parachute operations training aboard Marine Corps Base Camp Pendleton.

COURAGE

Throughout their history, the Marines have fought in battles where the odds against them seemed overwhelming. What they need are men and women who will not crack under pressure even when things seem desperate. Courage is not, as some people think, the absence of fear. Everyone feels afraid at some point; we're all human. Some think of

What Is Courage?

"If we take the generally accepted definition of bravery as a quality which knows no fear, I have never seen a brave man. All men are frightened."

—George S. Patton

"Courage is endurance for one moment more...."

—Unknown Marine Second Lieutenant in Vietnam

Marines as superhuman beings who do not feel normal emotions. In fact, they simply have the determination to go onward a little further.

The Marines look for people who show courage in their daily lives, such as standing up for what they feel is right even when everybody else might be against them. Courage is vital because if soldiers do not do their duty in combat, other people's lives may be lost.

Marines and civilians with the Command Financial Specialist Training course research pay information during a case study assignment. The group case study involved much of what the students learned during the week-long course.

KNOWLEDGE

One of the duties of a U.S. Marine is to become a "Lifelong Student of the Art of War." The Marines want all their soldiers to be well informed about military history, tactics, international politics, and foreign cultures, as well as know how to fight. That's why all Marines devote a lot of time to reading. They read about how other military leaders have fought wars, and how others have endured in battle. Knowledge of foreign people, places, and languages is also valuable. This knowledge allows soldiers to operate more easily on foreign operations in places very different from their homeland.

RESISTANCE TO PHYSICAL PAIN AND DISCOMFORT

The Marine's powers of endurance must be formidable by anybody's standards. Marines must be able to withstand

THE INTELLIGENT CORPS

The old image of the Marines as mindless warriors who thoughtlessly obey orders is totally out of date. Today's Marines must be intelligent and strong-minded, which is the reason why their basic training program is so demanding. They must be capable of thinking for themselves, and working out how to solve problems without asking others.

Up Is Down / Black Is White

When you first enter training, the way that things are done may not make complete sense to you, in fact many things will seem upside down. Your instructor may ask you to perform a task that makes no logical sense to you. Try your best not to go into special training with any preconceived ideas of what your lifestyle should be like. Expectations get in the way of experience, and in this case, the ability to adapt to your new circumstances. It is very important to keep a sense of distance from your experience during boot camp. Remind yourself that this experience is only temporary. Keeping up a healthy sense of humor and letting the small stuff go are both highly effective strategies that make boot-camp easier.

running or walking long distances. They must be able to continue fighting even if they have been wounded or have had no sleep for a week. They must be prepared for the capture and violent interrogation that threatens all elite operatives. This is why Marine training is so tough. The drill instructors want

LOOSE ENDS

If you have any emotional issues with people close to you such as parents or significant others, you should try your best to resolve them before going to camp. Training is stressful enough without having to worry about a problem with a relationship.

Marines prepare to evacuate a mock casualty during a mock helicopter raid at Camp Lejeune, North Carolina. The Helicopter Raid Course is one of several Special Operations Training Group, II Marine Expeditionary Force events as part of Twenty-Sixth Marine Expeditionary Unit's preparation for deployment.

to see who can push themselves to keep going even when their bodies feels like they want to stop. If they cannot keep pushing themselves through the pain of a long-distance run with 80 pounds (36 kg) of kit on their backs, then they will probably not have the strength to keep fighting in combat. Only when mental endurance is proven can units have the confidence that their Marines will never give in to adversity.

TEAM SPIRIT

However much Marines must stand on their own two feet, they must always think of others before themselves. A self-ish person will not do well as a Marine. In combat, soldiers must always have confidence in the people next to them. If they do not, then they will not trust each other and will not work together to achieve their mission. If this happens, then the mission will almost certainly fail. True Marines must look after their fellow soldiers as if they were broth-ers or sisters. The bonds between Marines are incredible. In many instances, Marines have been known to give their lives while trying to recover the dead bodies of their comrades. This commitment to each other is vital if they are to fight together in battle.

These are just some of the mental qualities demanded of the U.S. Marines, qualities that make them the unique soldiers they are. The will to never give up produces Marines who will stay brave and focused despite the danger all around them.

Five Reasons Why People Fail Boot Camp

The following are a common list of misconceptions and bad attitudes about boot camp. Try to do the opposite of these things:

- *Lack of preparation*: You may think you have worked out enough because you went to the gym a few months prior to starting boot camp, but the physical fitness required to be a Marine does not come quickly.

- *Lack of a personal drive*: It is important to always remember why you joined the Marines. Write down the number-one reason you are joining the military and always look at it while you are in boot camp. This should guide you through difficult times.

- *Lack of tenacity*: A drill sergeant is not there to be pleasant. They are there to break down any attitudes or assumptions about the military. Their goal is to shock you into military life. They want to form you into a soldier so that you will be prepared when it is time to perform for your country.

- *Lack of prior knowledge*: You will have a rush of new information when you join boot camp. A "smart book" will be handed to you once you get to basic training. The smart book includes: marching procedures, a phonetic alphabet, and other military traditions. Knowing these things ahead of time will give you an edge. Especially important may be: knowing the phonetic alphabet, knowing general orders, and understanding how to read military time. If Woody Allen was right when he said, "80 percent of success is showing up," then the other 20 percent is preparation. This leads us to the final reason why trainees fail boot camp.

- *Lack of mental preparation*: Not being in a good state of mind is the easiest way to fail boot camp, even easier than not being prepared physically. Being prepared in your mind ahead of time goes even farther than the other four reasons on this list. If you know that you have made the right decision and you never lose sight of that purpose, then the different obstacles appearing in your path won't seem so difficult to overcome. Once you are prepared in your mind, you are already partly there. Waking up at five in the morning, being screamed at, your face landing square into the mud-filled ground: these things seem less terrible when you are mentally prepared.

CHAPTER 3
Training and Selection

There are some basic requirements for joining the Marines. To join you must:

- be a U.S. citizen or a resident alien.
- be between the ages of 17 and 29. A seventeen-year-old needs the consent of his or her parents.
- have a high school diploma.
- pass a Military Entrance Processing Station medical exam.
- pass the Armed Services Vocational Aptitude Battery (ASVAB) test.

Women are able to join all fields except special infantry and artillery forces. Also tank and amphibian crewmembers must be male.

WHAT IT TAKES TO JOIN

Before they can become a Marine, recruits must convince their recruiters that they are suitable. Then they must survive the training program, one of the toughest in the world.

All Marine recruits have a long interview before they are allowed to begin training. First, recruits are tested for their level of physical toughness. But they are also assessed for their character and personality. Marine recruiters will probe deeply into the applicants' histories to find moments of courage, determination, or leadership, which may indicate what they will be like as a future Marine. If the individual has struggled through poverty to gain a good education or support a family, this might indicate strength of mind. If

Stress Training

Being mentally prepared is important to performance, both during training and during deployment. Studies have found that if you learn how to cope with stress before you enter the battlefield, you will be more likely to live a normal life during your tour of service and after. Studies have also found that a significantly larger number of troops that did not go through mental training suffered from larger levels of stress than those who were trained to manage stress.

the person has a criminal record, he or she will be rejected immediately; Marines must respect society and people.

Company E Marines climb the ropes under the supervision of their senior drill instructors during an obstacle course. The Marines climb the rope in flak jackets and Kevlar helmets in order to complete the course.

Marines from the Thirteenth Marine Expeditionary Unit (MEU) aboard USS Boxer perform weapons training drills on the flight deck. USS Boxer conducts training exercises in the Pacific Ocean in preparation for deployment.

Gradually, the recruiter will come to understand the people being interviewed, and form a judgment as to whether they are suited to be a Marine. Though they may have strong characters, they must also display another mental quality demanded by the Marine: intelligence. All Marines take long intelligence tests. Theses test skills such as English and mathematics. All Marines must show above-average scores from the tests, making them one of the most intelligent military units in the world.

The Marines also need people in control of their emotions. People who are violent, unpredictable, or unsociable will never make good Marines. However, neither do the Marines want people who do not give enough effort. Elite forces' missions tend to require high levels of aggressive commitment. Marines have to have flexible minds that can work out a problem, but they also must pursue their missions with total dedication. This is the quality we call "mental endurance," and it is this which is tested during training.

For the Marine, there is no such thing as "basic" training. Entering the Marines requires that soldiers undergo

MARINES AT ARMS

Marines are given their own M16 rifle when they join. This rifle goes almost everywhere with them. Because they become so familiar with this weapon, they have total confidence that they will know how to use it in battle. Soldiers who are not as well trained will not be able to fire their weapon as accurately in combat.

incredible physical punishment. For twelve weeks they will be shouted at, forced to run many miles with heavy packs on their backs, deprived of sleep for days at a time, and have to make decisions almost every waking minute. During that time, the candidates are watched to see what their characters are like. The drill instructors are looking for particular qualities.

TENACITY

Can soldiers keep focused on succeeding even when they are physically and mentally at the limits of their endurance? To see whether they can, they are put through exhausting marches and physical tasks. If they do these without complaining and with lots of effort, they will earn the drill instructor's approval.

INTELLIGENCE

Can soldiers solve problems quickly, even when they are under severe pressure? If they can't, then they wont be any good for the Marines. The ability to think clearly is made more difficult when you are extremely tired or exhausted. This is why the Marine drill instructors push the limits of the soldier's physical endurance, and then see if they are still capable of forming **tactical** decisions on the battlefield.

UNDERSTAND THE FULL MEANING

tactical: Referring to decision-making strategies that lead to successful outcomes.

TEAM SPIRIT

Do the candidates help other people succeed and put their own interests second? There is no place in the Marines for those who don't want to cooperate with other people.

A rifleman with Company I, Battalion Landing Team 3/8, 26th Marine Expeditionary Unit, sights in on a target during a squad exercise. During this eighteen-day training evolution, the MEU will conduct several types of exercises as part of training before deployment.

BASIC TRAINING

The U.S. Marines' basic training period is designed to be as punishing and demanding as possible. This is because potential recruits may be able to pretend that they are tough for a couple of days, but over a grueling twelve-week period they will not have enough stamina to keep on pretending. During the twelve weeks, the Marine officers will be able to assess the recruit's true character.

Team players will also tend to make better tactical thinkers because they ask other people for their opinions rather than assume that they themselves know best.

SELF-CONTROL

Do the candidates show they can control their emotions at all times? Marine training often involves two drill instructors shouting different sets of orders at a confused and bewildered recruit. The purpose of this is not to taunt the recruit. Instead, the instructors are watching how he reacts. If he loses his temper and cannot make a decision about what to do, then he will probably not be right for making decisions on the battlefield. However, if he keeps his head, thinks clearly, then makes a decision, this will show the instructors he has self-control.

How to Handle Panic

A psychiatrist in Japan created a three-step exercise that helps his patients cope with panic. It can easily be applied when dealing with the stress that comes with applying for the special forces and training as well. The three steps are:

- Stand or sit upright.
- Take a deep breath through the mouth, filling your lungs.
- Exhale very slowly through the nose. Imagine that you are holding a feather in front of your nose and exhale so gently that the "feather" remains perfectly still.

SENSE OF HUMOR

Does the candidate have a sense of humor? This is not just welcome in the Marine Corps; it is essential. Studies conducted during the Korean War found that soldiers with a sense of humor tended to make better fighters. This was because they did not crack under pressure so much, and they improved **morale** in their units.

UNDERSTAND THE FULL MEANING

morale: The mental outlook, positive or negative, of an individual or group of individuals.

Staff Sergeant Ryan Smith, the Public Affairs Chief with Headquarters Company, Regimental Combat Team (RCT) Eight, pitches a baseball to a Marine with RCT Eight's Mobile Security Detachment (MSD) during a baseball game. The MSD Marines organized the game and cookout to boost camaraderie and morale within the platoon.

Training for the Marine Corps is so tough that by the end of the twelve weeks, about 20 percent of the recruits will have been rejected. The reasons for this are clear. The Marines are an elite unit. They want only the best because

Keeping a Sense of Humor

Corporal Charles Brown shows the importance of keeping a sense of humor. He is stationed in Okinawa, Japan, and uses his sense of humor to "brighten everyone's day," greeting each person during his two hours of standing duty outside an operations center. Most people would see standing duty as a boring chore, but Brown sees it as an opportunity to brighten another soldier's day. While he uses humor to keep things light with other troops, he knows the reason he is there: to defend his country. "People need a little light humor sometimes, especially out here," he said. "But if any bad guys try any funny stuff while I'm on duty, I'll be all over them like a rat on a Cheeto."

they need to uphold the reputation that they have earned over two hundred years of constantly striving.

Most Marines will tell you that it is the proudest moment of their lives when they finally go from being recruits to being Marines. Life in the Marine Corps is never easy, but wearing the Marine Corps uniform means that they have become a member of the Marine family for the rest of their lives. It also shows that they have the character to succeed in the face of hardship and punishment.

CHAPTER 4

Missions Around the World

Currently the Marines dedicate their time and energy to the war in Afghanistan. They also participate in providing aid in humanitarian crises around the world.

MILITARY MISSIONS: AFGHANISTAN

In September 30, 2001, President Bush stated in a speech about Afghanistan, "They will hand over the terrorists or they will share in their fate." It was well known that Osama Bin Laden was in Afghanistan at the time. The Taliban refused to release Bin Laden. Operation Enduring Freedom (the official name for the war in Afghanistan) had begun.

In Afghanistan, the Marines were used to root out Taliban forces from heavily populated areas. The Marines have been in the war since the beginning of the conflict. The U.S. Military deployed the Marines first, and the Marines saw the first signs of heavy combat in November of 2001. While supported by heavy airstrikes, the Marines took the Taliban out of power in the major cities and areas of Afghanistan.

In the winter of 2003 the Taliban began regrouping and began what we call an insurgency, an armed effort from a small group of people to attack the government or occupation in power. The Taliban was regrouping, and planning on taking power back. The War in Iraq became a bigger story in the media at this time, but the conflict in Afghanistan never stopped. By 2009, the war in Afghanistan became more prominent again, and 2009 saw the worst U.S. casualties in Afghanistan since the conflict had begun eight years earlier. President Obama ordered a large increase in the number of troops deployed in Afghanistan by the end of 2010.

The Marines have had success in rooting insurgents out of major cities but there was more work to be done. The following stories are a taste of what being a Marine is like in Afghanistan.

INVASION OF MARJA

The Marines participated in Operation Moshtarak, one of the largest military operations since the initial invasion. The mission was to take over much of the land dominated by the Taliban and drug dealers. The production and sale of poppy plants in Afghanistan is one of the biggest elements of the local economy. Poppies make opium and heroin, which is the main source of income for 60 to 70 percent of farmers in the south of Afghanistan. Money from poppy sales makes billions of dollars for extremists in Afghanistan. Besides the poppy seed problem, the Taliban had a stronghold in a major city there, Marja.

A Marine invading Marja would deal with the constant threat of **IED**s (roadside bombs) as they entered. These bombs are common, but Marine forces reported a larger than usual network of booby traps and bombs as they entered the city. To get through the trap the Marines used special mine-clearing vehicles, clearing minefields and other bombs. Many Marines deployed into Marja by the V-22 Osprey, a special military aircraft that looks like a combination of a helicopter and small airplane.

The gunfire the troops saw on the battleground in Marja was scary enough, but even worse were Afghani snipers who hid from sight. Joshua T. Hurst, a Marine who participated in the invasion of Marja, talks about the experience of entering the warzone: "We started taking small-arms and indirect fire from every direction. Rounds were cracking over our heads. . . . When the snipers started to shoot, my frustrations reached their peak. [I was] thinking, 'If I move an inch I'm going to get shot.'"

Once the bombs had been cleared and the first wave of shooting was done, the Marines quickly tried to maintain power in the area. Once the Marines were in Marja, the tension level was high.

UNDERSTAND THE FULL MEANING

IED: Improvised Explosive Device: homemade bombs used in Iraq and Afghanistan.

James R. Borzillieri, a gunner who participated in the operation, spoke to a reporter about the need to be adaptable. "The only thing that really prepped me for this deployment was my last. Nothing you can do to prepare, except do it. . . . Trying to prepare for combat, you need to understand that you can't control who gets hit or who's coming back. You just have to keep your head down and fire back. Keeping your composure is key."

The Marines successfully took over Marja from the Taliban, a major victory in the war after a series of setbacks. General Charles Hudson stated that Operation Moshtarak was an event "that will go down in Marine Corps history." However, as the next section shows, winning the battle is only half the war.

FOOD FOR PEACE

Many of the Marines who survived ferocious shootouts and dodged IEDs on crater-filled roads were ordered to fulfill a very different mission. The U.S. Marines and Afghani Army made sure they could hold on to power now that they had uprooted the Taliban. To do this they needed to address the drug problem in Afghanistan. If they destroyed all poppy crops without giving villagers another crop to farm, however, it would destroy the civilians' lives and turn them against the American occupation. Instead, the Marines worked to help the local population so they did not have to produce poppy plants.

Marines in Marja helped the farmers cope with a difficult harvesting season. A bitter winter in 2010 destroyed many crops. This could have influenced these citizens to grow the drug-producing plants, but he Marines gave 50 kilograms (110.8 lbs.) of radishes, beans, sesame seeds, and other crops to each farmer. This plan was good for everyone: the farmers could make a decent living without having to give

Lance Cpl. Jeremy Fasci, assists a Marja resident place a bag of fertilizer onto a wheelbarrow at the Civil-Military Operations Center at Camp Hansen, Marja, Afghanistan. The food zone program, led by the Helmand Provincial Reconstruction Team, distributed more than 1,066 packages of fertilizer and seeds to farmers throughout northern Marja

Sign of the Times

It was a scene considered impossible until recently. On May 9, 2010, U.S. soldiers marched in front of the Kremlin in Russia in a celebration of their victory over the Nazis during World War II. Less than thirty years earlier, U.S. President Ronald Reagan called the USSR an "evil empire." The Soviet Union collapsed in 1990, bringing a changing reality for the U.S. Military. At that time, the U.S. Military spent millions on weapons hoping to beat the Russians in an arms race. Now, the war on terror is at the forefront of the military's efforts.

U.S. troops marching in Moscow is a sign that things have changed. When we currently read the news or talk about politics, we don't usually fear a single enemy country as a threat; instead, we see loose groups of terrorists using lethal weapons as the greatest threat to our national security. The Marines have updated their thinking, responding to the new threat by taking the war to enemy lines. We now use the Marines to not only support other factions in major military conflicts but also in performing special missions to respond to rogue groups in other countries. in other words, the major military conflicts are increasingly fought against small networks of extremists rather than a single country with defined borders.

While relations with Russia have been strained since former President Vladimir Putin made a speech critical of the U.S. in 2007, both countries cooperate together. Other former rivals in the Cold War—including China and even Vietnam—have now warmed to the United States. Russian President Medvedev has stated that only by standing together can we prevent the threat of war.

crops to a drug-lord, while the U.S. Military won over citizens who could have just as easily handed money and loyalty to the Taliban.

MEETING WITH TRIBESMEN

In Koshtay Village in Afghanistan, a group of recently deployed Marines are meeting with local tribes. They sit on a long roll of blue carpet swapping ideas and beliefs about the war. The tribesmen want to be secure but they also want something else: schools. Since the invasion of Afghanistan in the 1970s, decent schools have not been built or maintained. Students learn from home or at a **mosque**. A study found that merely 28 percent of Afghanis are **literate**. To put this into context, bordering country Iran has a literacy rate of 82 percent and another neighboring country, Pakistan has a literacy rate of 49 percent.

The American Marines are building trust with villagers. One of the biggest goals of the U.S. Army is to help the government in Afghanistan win the trust of its own population. In December of 2010, 60 out of 121 regions in Afghanistan either supported or were neutral to their government. By March, that number of regions rose to 73. None of the regions fully favored the U.S. military presence or their allies.

The Marines are meeting with local tribesmen to change that. They know they need more civilians to support their own government and not aid the Taliban. Being a Marine in

UNDERSTAND THE FULL MEANING

mosque: Place of worship for a Muslim.

literate: Able to read and write.

Afghanistan requires bravery under fire, but it also requires the ability to win trust.

CULTURAL TRAINING

The Marines now take classes on Afghani culture. They are hoping that by learning facts on the ground about the people they will be dealing with, they can win over more of the local population. Mohammad Azamy, a native Afghan, taught the Marines the religion, language, and customs of Afghanistan. Azamy taught that *wasta*—a word that means respect—was important to Afghan society. Elders are figures of high-respect and outsiders are expected to act as the locals do to them. Azamy also taught the Marines about the daily life of Afghans, as well as the personal experiences and outlook of the people with whom the Marines interact each day when they are deployed.

The time devoted in a classroom could be spent learning newer survival techniques, but the military focuses on cultural training for a good reason. These Marines will represent America to the people with whom they deal each day. If a Marine makes a good impression on a local, that could be the difference between an ally and an enemy. The Afghan public would remember signs of disrespect or any rudeness toward their traditions. Lieutenant Matthew Fallon, officer for a unit being trained, made a strong point: "These kids are going to have more influence on American policy than most diplomats do in Washington, D.C."

During a village medical outreach outside Naw-Abad, First Lt. Justine Roberts, public affairs officer with I Marine Expeditionary Force (FWD), shows the children how to use a jump rope. Marines and medical officers from Brigade Headquarters Group and Third Low Altitude Air Defense Battalion, I MEF (FWD) and an Afghan National Army medic from Camp Shorabak, set up and conducted the outreach to provide medical care and assess long term medical needs.

BUILDING HOSPITALS IN HAITI

The Marines do not just wage war against America's enemies; they also help those in crisis. Historically, the Marines have been first to intervene during natural disasters. In the beginning of 2010, the island country of Haiti suffered from a strong earthquake. It was the sixth deadliest earthquake ever recorded, up to 300,000 Haitians died. One million victims of the earthquake became homeless; this is comparable to the entire population of Montana not knowing where they will sleep the next day.

Marine Battalion 24 began to build medical facilities on January 31, 2010. The Marines built a city of army-green tents within two days. Close to a hundred Marines and sailors, as well as U.S. Army soldiers, transported tents, food, and water. The three branches of the military worked together to provide relief for Haiti. The Navy gave medical care, the Army transported supplies, and the Marines provided security.

PIRATES!

The Marines also perform military operations outside of conventional warfare. In 2010, President Barack Obama called upon the Marines and Navy to rescue an American hostage from Somali pirates.

Pirating has come back as a serious danger for many around the Horn of Africa, which is in the easternmost part

The lifeboat from the Maersk Alabama is hoisted aboard the amphibious assault ship USS Boxer to be processed for evidence after the successful rescue of Capt. Richard Phillips. Somali pirates held Phillips hostage in the lifeboat on the Indian Ocean for five days after a failed hijacking attempt off the Somali coast.

of Africa. It is the southern part of the Somali Peninsula. More than 120 pirate attacks occurred near this area in 2008, and pirates have stolen more than $100 million dollars in various illegal activities around the area. One of the most profitable ways of making money is to hold for ransom important passengers of the ships they board. One of the Somali pirates' greatest successes was taking a Ukrainian freighter packed with tanks, antiaircraft guns, and other weapons. After four months, the Ukrainian government paid over three million dollars to get the ship back. This was not an unusual occurrence; it was the twenty-sixth attack in the area in 2008. What was unusual was the effectiveness of the pirates in getting what they wanted.

But they didn't get what they wanted when they took Captain Richard Phillips hostage in April 2010. After the pirates repeatedly threatened to kill the captain if the U.S. government did not pay money, President Obama authorized the Marines and Navy to use force if necessary.

It was a standoff. Then the pirates began to run out of food, water, and fuel. Eventually one of the pirates surrendered because of an injured hand. Another dramatic moment occurred when Captain Phillips tried to escape by jumping out of a lifeboat on April 10th, but the pirates recaptured him.

On the evening of April 12th, two of Phillips' captors poked their heads out of the lifeboat; the third was visible from a window in the bow. He was pointing an automatic rifle at Captain Phillips. It was the perfect opportunity for American snipers who were watching.

Three snipers fired at three men at night. All three men were shot down. The captain was now free.

TRAINING LOCAL FORCES

Corruption has been a problem in Afghanistan for quite some time. John Scheider, a Marine training the police there, said, "The local police that were in Marja a couple years back were very corrupt, they would tax people, abuse their authority and steal." One of the most difficult tasks for the Marines is to help the police win the trust of the local population. Also, many of the police in Afghanistan have not yet learned to be self-sufficient; they cannot yet defend Afghanistan without the help of the United States.

To help them achieve self-sufficiency, the police force goes through a three-week course with the Marines. Marine Caleb Love, who was a part of the training operation, said, "All they really know is about searching personnel and vehicles. We try and advance them, train them on how to question people, gather **intelligence**, process **detainees**, and the paperwork side of things, but the biggest thing we're trying to teach them is self reliance."

Elsewhere, in Africa, the Marines are training Malian military units how to best defend against Al Qaeda. It is

UNDERSTAND THE FULL MEANING

intelligence: Information about the activities of an enemy force.
detainees: Civilians held in custody for questioning or as security risks.

Afghan National Police prepare to graduate from the police academy at the ANP headquarters in Herat, Afghanistan. The graduates were among thousands of police being added to the ANP in order to raise the number of Afghan police from its current 81,000 to 160,000 by 2013.

estimated that four hundred heavily armed Islamic militants have set up base in Mali. Major Cheikhna Dieng stated, "The point is, we've got to start getting ready for al-Qaida if they come our way. The army of Mali is dangerously underfunded and its troops would not have had the resources to combat Al Qaeda forces." That's why the Marines are there, along with other Special Forces units: to train the Malian army. Shane West, a Special Forces officer training the Malians, said, "We're essentially here to help our host nation handle whatever situation it needs to. . . . And we're taking it step by step."

These examples show that not everything the Marines do is on the battlefield!

TOMORROW'S ARMY

Secretary of Defense Robert Gates has spoken of the need to update the Army. The old wars of the twentieth century are quite different from the wars America has participated in so far during the twenty-first century. For instance, during World War II, the U.S. Military fought with tanks against tanks across a clearly defined battleground. If the United States captured a part of Nazi land, they continued on until the enemy surrendered—and then the battle was done. In the Iraq and Afghanistan wars, however, the United States was more than capable of destroying the governments that were in power at the time. For instance, in March 2003, the United States began the invasion of Iraq. By May 2003,

President Bush declared in a speech, "fellow Americans: Major combat operations in Iraq have ended."

However, the war was not over. It was not until December of 2003 that Saddam Hussein was captured, and the worst bloodshed of the war did not stop until years later. The war in Iraq truly began only after the invasion, when many insur-

Mommy Marine

Lisa Strickland has a nineteen-month-old daughter named Avalon Rose. Each day she wakes up at six in the morning to take care of her daughter before going off to work. The difference between her and any other young mother? Lisa is a Marine.

Lisa is married to a Marine as well. They are what are called, "dual-military families." Both Lisa and her husband are worried about being deployed at the same time. Lisa hasn't had to leave her children yet, but the time is coming up. She will be deployed in Afghanistan and her husband will take care of their daughter on his own. Although she wished that she didn't have to be separated from her daughter, Lisa had no regrets about choosing the two hardest jobs in the world—motherhood and the Marines. "Would I do it any other way? No."

gent forces attacked the United States military. The war in Afghanistan followed a similar pattern. Operation Enduring Freedom began with American airplanes pounding the Taliban, and Marines taking enemy forces down with great precision. Many rebel forces emerged from defeat, however,

Post-Traumatic Stress Disorder

Every casualty is not suffered on the battlefield, and not all wounds are visible. Many soldiers in the military deal with Post-Traumatic Stress Disorder (PTSD), Marines are no exception. PTSD is any condition that occurs after a stressful event such as sleeping problems, withdrawal from society, or constantly fixating on a traumatic event. The frequency of PTSD is staggering; psychiatrists estimate that up to one in three U.S. soldiers who served in Iraq or Afghanistan may develop this condition. Even more shocking than the large numbers of people that develop the condition are the small numbers of those who will be treated. Only 50 percent of veterans will get the treatment that they need. Sadly, we know that many who are not treated drink or do drugs to numb the pain. The number of veterans reporting PTSD is rising past the resources available to treat it. One of the worst attributes of the PTSD problem is the strong feeling among veterans of misguided shame. Many wrongfully think there is something wrong with them if they suffer depression. Soldiers are trained to keep their head up and perform their duty on the battlefield. Not being able to keep a positive attitude due to mental health problems is especially damaging to veterans. But despite these emotional challenges, our Marines still have the spirit of warriors.

to be a major thorn in the side of the American presence in Afghanistan.

Secretary Gates fully understands that a new type of war has emerged. In the new conflicts, there is a great need to build trust with local governments and give these governments the training and materials needed to fight against insurgents. Gates states. "Possessing the ability to annihilate other militaries is no guarantee we can achieve our strategic goals—a point driven home especially in Iraq."

Tomorrow's Marines will learn to adapt to a new type of war, one where the line between what was called "conventional warfare" (fighting across a battlefield with clearly-defined land) and "unconventional warfare" (fighting against a hidden enemy in urban areas, training local forces, winning hearts and minds) has become increasingly blurred. Gates states, "You must continue to be the **visionaries**, the pathfinders, the . . . cutting edge."

This is the mission the Marines face today.

UNDERSTAND THE FULL MEANING

visionaries: People whose imagination and courage help shape the future.

FIND OUT MORE ON THE INTERNET

Air Force www.airforce.com

Army Recruiting www.goarmy.com

Department of Defense www.defense.gov

Marine Corps www.marines.com

Navy www.navy.com

U.S. Naval Academy www.usna.edu

West Point www.usma.edu

The websites listed on this page were active at the time of publication. The publisher is not responsible for websites that have changed their address or discontinued operation since the date of publication. The publisher will review and update the websites upon each reprint.

FURTHER READING

Couch, Dick. *Chosen Soldier: The Making of a Special Forces Warrior.* New York, N.Y.: Three Rivers Press, 2007.

David, Jack. *Marine Corps Force Recon.* Minneapolis, Minn.: Bellwether Media, 2009.

De Lisle, Mark. *Special Ops Fitness Training: High-Intensity Workouts of Navy Seals, Delta Force, Marine Force Recon and Army Rangers.* Berkeley, Calif.: Ulysses Press, 2008.

Martin, Iain C. *The Greatest U.S. Marine Corps Stories Ever Told: Unforgettable Stories of Courage, Honor, and Sacrifice.* Guilford, Conn.: The Lyons Press, 2007.

Martin, Joseph J. *Get Selected! for Special Forces: How to Successfully Train for and Complete Special Forces Assessment & Selection.* Warrior-Mentor.com, 2005.

Stein, R. Conrad. *The U.S. Marine Corps and Military Careers.* Berkeley Heights, N.J.: Enslow Publishers, 2005.

BIBILIOGRAPHY

Associated Press, "Mullen Says Kandahar Campaign Will Take Months," www.npr.org/templates/story/story.php?storyId=103363131 (1 June 2010).

Dwyer, Devin, "2009 Deadliest Year for U.S. in Afghanistan," abcnews.go.com/Politics/2009-deadliest-year-us-afghanistan/story?id=9457231 (26 May 2010).

ENCToday.com, "Lejeune troops learn to win hearts, minds in Afghanistan," www.enctoday.com/news/troops-78176-jdn-afghanistan-morning.html (27 May 2010).

Haaretz.com, "WWII Allies march in Moscow to mark 65 years since Nazi defeat," www.haaretz.com/news/international/wwii-allies-march-in-moscow-to-mark-65-years-since-nazi-defeat-1.289202 (2 June 2010).

Jaroncyk, Ryan, "After Nearly a Decade of War, PTSD Is Afflicting the U.S. Military," caivn.org/article/2010/05/10/after-nearly-decade-war-ptsd-afflicting-us-military (26 May 2010).

McCarthy, Terry, "'Thundering Third' Meet with Local Afghan Leaders," www.cbsnews.com/8301-503543_162-20004215-503543.html (1 June 2010).

Odd Facts That Happen To Be True, "Odd But True Facts About World War Two," luckypuppyoddfacts.com/WWII.html (2 June 2010).

United States Marine Corps, "Combat Logistics Battalion 1 Marines, Sailors 'Will Go Down in Marine Corps History,' General Says," www.

marines.mil/unit/1stmlg/Pages/CombatLogisticsBattalion1Marines, Sailors%27willGoDowninMarineCorpsHistory,%27GeneralSays.aspx (27 May 2010).

———, "Marines provide Marjah farmers with fertilizer, seeds during crucial harvest season," www.marines.mil/unit/imef/Pages/Marinesp rovideMarjahfarmerswithfertilizer,seedsduringcrucialharvest season.aspx (28 May 2010).

———, "Three long days, nights; The first 72 hours in Marjah with 1/6 mortarmen," www.marines.mil/unit/hqmc/Pages/Threelongdaysand nights;Thefirst72hoursinMarjahwith16mortarmen.aspx (27 May 2010).

INDEX

ABOUT THE AUTHOR

Jack Montana lives in upstate New York with his wife and three dogs. He writes on military survival, health, and wellness. He graduated from Binghamton University.

ABOUT THE CONSULTANT

Colonel John Carney, Jr., is USAF-Ret President and the CEO of the Special Operations Warrior Foundation.

PICTURE CREDITS

U.S. Marines: pp. 8, 30
    Cpl. Christopher O'Quin: p. 21
    Lance Cpl. Christopher O'Quin: p. 23
    Lance Cpl. Claudio A. Martinez: p. 18
    Lance Cpl. Megan Sindelar: p. 51
    Lance Cpl. Santiago G. Colon Jr.: p. 37
    Lance Corporal Tammy Hineline: p. 26
    Pfc. Katalynn Thomas: p. 33
    Sgt. Dean Davis: p. 15
    Sgt. Eric C. Schwartz: p. 40

Sgt. Mark Fayloga: p. 42
Staff Sgt. Luis R. Agostini: p. 47

National Archives and Records Administration (NARA): p. 13

U.S. Department of Defense:
    Mass Communication Specialist 2nd Class Jon Rasmussen: p. 53
    Mass Communication Specialist 3rd Class Daniel Barker: p. 34
    Sgt. Stephen Decatur: p. 56

To the best knowledge of the publisher, all images not specifically credited are in the public domain. If any image has been inadvertently uncredited, please notify Harding House Publishing Service, 220 Front Street, Vestal, New York 13850, so that credit can be given in future printings.